Paul M. Carlson

Where are my Feet?

Searching *for* Solid Ground

WHERE ARE MY FEET?

SEARCHING FOR SOLID GROUND

PAUL CARLSON

LYONS INK PUBLISHING

Lyons Ink Publishing
Oregon, USA

Published by Lyons Ink Publishing, a division of Grit and Grace Enterprises

eBook ISBN: 979-8-9932720-2-3
Paperback ISBN: 979-8-9932720-3-0
Library of Congress Control Number: 2025924368

First Edition

Book Production and Publishing Setup by Lyons Ink Publishing

www.gritandgraceenterprises.com

www.gritandgraceenterprises.com

Lyons Ink-Author-Written
REAL
AUTHOR VOICE
SEAL™
HUMAN CRAFTED
STORY-DRIVEN

This one is for you, Don.

Contents

Preface

Like so many others, my life has been full of twists, turns, and unexpected detours. Sometimes I think of it as the most amazing roller coaster ever built and then set on fire halfway through the ride.

While much of my life has been relatively simple, the years following 2020 pushed me into a season of self-reflection, growth, and change unlike anything I'd experienced before.

This book is a collection of what I've learned along the way. Each chapter is rooted in a principle I wrestled with—sometimes gracefully, sometimes stubbornly—and breaks big ideas into smaller, more digestible pieces. Not because I have all the answers, but because I finally started asking the right questions.

Note to the Reader

A global pandemic. Depression. Not showing up. Failing the people who relied on me. And perhaps worst of all—failing myself.

Not exactly the ingredients of an uplifting book, I know. But each of those things played a role in how I got here.

This book takes simple ideas I've learned over the years, simplifying them into the lessons that shaped my growth during one of the most challenging seasons of my life. I wouldn't call it an autobiography; it's more like a tourist's guide to life and recovery, told from my limited but hard-earned perspective.

This journey really began when I finally accepted something I'd avoided for far too long: the biggest problem in my life was me. And the only person who could change the direction I was headed was also me. I couldn't become the father, husband, friend, or employee I was meant to be without drawing on the wisdom of others and having the willingness to dig deep and change.

As I started doing that work, I began to realize something. Just as others had shared their experience and guidance with me, it was now my turn to share what I was learning. I'm not smarter than anyone else, and my life hasn't been harder than most, but not everyone has walked this exact road or been lucky enough to encounter the people I did.

Many of the ideas and lessons in this book came from my friend and sponsor. I still couldn't tell you how he ended up in my life, but I thank God every day that he did. To protect his anonymity, I'll refer to him simply as the "Godfather." That nickname is fitting for a lot of reasons—and to the best of my knowledge has nothing to do with actual mob ties, though with his past, I wouldn't be shocked!

To the Godfather—and to the therapists, coaches, personal trainers, friends, and family who walked with me through the hardest chapters of my life—I dedicate this book to you. If not for your help, and the thought of not being here for my three children, I wouldn't be here at all.

So why write this? Why share all of this? Why lay my story bare?

Because not everyone gets the opportunity to dig deep, ask hard questions, and rebuild. Not everyone takes the same paths I walked. And not everyone has been blessed with the support and guidance I received.

I hope sharing this journey helps someone else face their own storm. I hope I can simplify these ideas in a way that's honest and clear. I hope the passion and conviction behind these pages come through. And most of all, I hope that something in here helps someone, or gives them something they can pass on to someone who looks up to them.

My hope is that something within these pages helps someone else the way all of you helped me.

The stories in this book are sincere and based on my best recollection. When possible, I've omitted or changed names out of respect for others.

It's with humility and deep gratitude that I begin.

PART I

THE WAKE-UP CALL

Sometimes we wake up in a life we don't even recognize, or one we were sleepwalking through. This part of the journey is full of hard truths, quiet breakdowns, and the first flickers of awareness. It's not comfortable, but it's where real change begins: in the asking, *how did I get here, and where are my feet now?*

Chapter 1

How Did We Get Here?

In the beginning, people think vulnerability will make you weak, but it does the opposite. It shows you're strong enough to care.

— Victoria Pratt

I found 2020 to be an interesting year, to say the least. A global pandemic hit, affecting every person on the planet. People got sick. People died. Families lost loved ones, jobs, incomes, and, in many cases, their sanity. Fear, isolation, and uncertainty spread faster than the virus itself. Depression, suicide, divorce, and addiction surged.

Not many of us were spared. And while my struggles paled in comparison to those of many others, I was no exception.

This book begins with the awakening I had late in 2020—an awakening that changed the course of my life forever. The process didn't happen overnight, and it's far from finished. But this is where it all began.

On November 3, 2020, while cooking a special dinner, I heard the words no spouse wants to hear:

"I am not happy. You are not happy. I don't love you anymore. There's no spark. I'm not attracted to you. I don't want to be with you."

Ironically, or karmically, I had once spoken those same words to someone else. I had stood on the other side of that moment, and now I was feeling the weight of the very pain I had once inflicted.

The road leading to that conversation was all too familiar. And what happened after was, in many ways, just as familiar. But this time, I was the one left standing in the ashes.

There were a thousand ways that moment a could have gone. And while I did some things right in the months that followed, I also did a lot wrong. Still, I ended up exactly where I was supposed to, not because I had the answers, but because I was finally asking the right questions.

The next morning, November 4, after almost no sleep, I looked in the mirror and asked myself the question that would change everything:

"Paul, what are you doing?"

There's only one common denominator in all the good times and all the bad in my life—*me.* My thoughts, my actions, my baggage, my decisions, my fears, my attitude—*me.* And if I wanted anything to change, I had to start—with *me.*

So I did. I set out on a course of physical, emotional, and spiritual recovery. Therapists. Doctors. Personal trainers. Coaches. Mentors. Accountability partners. Meetings. I built a team to help me find the man who used to live inside this worn-out meat shell I was dragging around.

I don't remember everything. Some moments I'd rather forget. Some I still can't make sense of. But I know this: the months between November

3, 2020, and today were the hardest, most painful, most transformative season of my life.

In June 2021, I found myself in a 12-step program after I realized that what I thought was my rock bottom had a basement. And not only did I go deeper—I needed to.

I was ready to go up, all the way to the top, but I learned the elevator was broken. The only way up was doing the steps.

So there I was. I had realized my life had become unmanageable. I could not keep going as I was. I had to admit that the problem I kept trying to outrun was me. Not the world. Not the people I blamed. Me.

I finally understood I could not fix this on my own. I needed something bigger than me. Like the moment when you quit pretending your headache will magically disappear and you finally take the aspirin you should have taken five hours earlier.

I made a decision. Not a clean decision, not a brave decision, but a decision to find the help I needed and listen to it. At least on the days I was able. At first, it was ugly. It was nothing more than a statement of intent with no muscle behind it. The follow-through was a doozy.

What came next? Where do you go after you admit you are the problem? If I had reached that conclusion when I was younger, I might have written a song and become famous, but I was late to the party. All I could do now was dig deep. And what did that even mean?

Well, at first, it was easy. I wrote down every single way every person in my life had ever wronged me. That felt great. Look at all the things they did to me. Their failures. Their betrayals. Their shortcomings. And then came the part I did not expect—I had to go back through the list and acknowledge the role I played.

Excuse me? My role? This exercise was supposed to be about them hurting me. What do you mean by defects of character? I am one of the greatest people I know. Just ask me, and I will tell you.

But the truth would not stay hidden. Every situation began with a decision I made. Every reaction was tied to something fractured inside me. I blamed others for taking advantage of my generosity, but it was because I lacked boundaries. When I felt used, it was because I refused to acknowledge my codependency. The resentment I carried came from my silence in moments when I should have spoken up. I had never looked at these patterns under a microscope, not like this.

Digging deep hurt. It was uncomfortable in ways I had never experienced. I had done surface work before, but this was different. This was the kind of work you feel in your ribs.

Once it was all on paper, the relief came in an unexpected way. I had to say it all out loud to another person. I had heard the phrase you are only as sick as your secrets, but I never understood it until that day. And it hit on two fronts.

First was the past, the things I had done that carried shame. The things that were done to me that I feared would destroy me if anyone knew. The choices I hid because they came with guilt and regret. And second was the future. If I wanted to keep my integrity, I could not live a life that required secrets. I had to make different choices. I had to think about how my actions affected others and not just my own selfish impulses.

The path that followed involved reaching out to the people I had wronged and owning my mistakes. It meant checking myself every day and correcting things as soon as I saw them. It meant helping others who were stuck in the same loop, which is part of why you are holding this book. I wrote all of this in hopes that someone will see themselves in these pages and step off the same merry-go-round I rode for years.

When I began writing in 2020, I never intended for anyone to read it. The first words were raw pain and anger. Finger pointing. Blame. None of it helped me. None of it would have helped anyone else.

So this is the truth of how we got here—the short version without the gory details. From here, you take each day as it comes. One step at a time, over and over.

You do the work, you keep showing up, and you climb the stairs.

PART II

THE MIRROR DOESN'T LIE

The mirror doesn't care about your excuses. This section is about self-inventory—not to shame, but to gain a deeper understanding of yourself. Here, we learn that healing doesn't begin with fixing others. It begins when we stop looking out the window and start looking inward.

CHAPTER 2

YOU SPOT IT, YOU GOT IT!

If I am unhappy with what I receive, I might try looking for that same behavior in myself. It may not take exactly the same form, but I find that whatever I dislike in another is something that I dislike in Myself. The reverse is also true: What I admire in others probably reflects an admirable quality within me.

— Courage to Change

We're often quick to point out the flaws in others while ignoring the mess in our own lives. I've been especially guilty of this, and honestly, I was appalled when I finally saw it clearly.

Who was I to play God and judge anyone? Why was I standing in a glass house, hurling stones? How could I see everyone else's side of the street while staying blind to my own?

This idea—*you spot it, you got it*—helped me take a deeper look at myself, but it also helped me understand others better. When I lashed out at someone, was I really just frustrated with something in myself? Was I avoiding my own work by highlighting what someone else was doing wrong?

I remember a conversation with a friend and colleague I hadn't seen since I started my recovery journey. After we caught up on business, he asked how I was doing personally. I'd already hit rock bottom and was clawing my way back up, so I decided to be honest. I shared some of what I'd been through. As I spoke, I could see the sadness grow in his eyes, and I found out why a little later.

About a week before that meeting, I had posted something on Facebook that sparked an argument at home. My motives were questioned. Was I being passive-aggressive? Spiteful? Trying to hurt someone or stir up attention?

In that moment, I really had to check myself. Were my motives selfish or sincere? Was I sharing from pain or from healing?

Later that day, my friend pulled me aside and said, "You recently posted something on social media. I haven't seen much from you in a while, but this one came through. I just need you to know that I needed to read that post. Right then, in that exact moment, it hit me hard because I've been going through stuff at home too."

He went on to open up about his own pain. His own confusion. His own storm. And in that conversation, I got to pass along a lesson that had helped me:

Sometimes the criticism people throw at you isn't really about you. It's about them.

For example, someone might say, "You're a horrible parent." That doesn't automatically mean you are. Sure, you can reflect and adjust if there's truth to it, but understand that they might be projecting their own struggle.

Maybe that Mom always dreamed of being involved in everything—the PTA meetings, class parties, lunchbox notes—but now she's working full time, running on fumes, and feeling like she's falling short. That shame might get redirected as judgment, to make her feel a little less alone.

We see this in relationships too. The cheating partner who accuses *you* of cheating? That's often projection. If I believe you've wronged me too, I can feel a little better about the wrong I'm doing.

Yes, sometimes there's deeper stuff at play, like personality disorders or mental health concerns, and I won't pretend to be an expert on that. But in many everyday situations, what we criticize in others is often what we struggle with.

So what do we do with comments like that? We pause. We reflect. And we stop treating someone else's opinion as fact.

I caught myself thinking my partner wasn't being a good wife. Maybe she was or maybe she wasn't. The truth was, however, *I* wasn't showing up as a good husband. And that's what mattered, because I'm the only person I can change.

It's also vital to remember that **someone's words about you are just that—their words.** Sit with them. Reflect. Determine whether they have something worthwhile for you to learn. But don't let them define who you are.

Another person's opinion is simply an opinion. In their version of reality, you may be the villain. But if I said you were an axe murderer, would that make it true? No, that's *my* belief, not *your* truth.

If you take only two things from this chapter, let it be this:

1. What others project onto you is often more about them than it is about you.
2. Someone else's version of you is not necessarily your reality.

CHAPTER 3

LET IT BEGIN WITH ME

We but mirror the world. All the tendencies present in the outer world are to be found in the world of our body. If we could change ourselves, the tendencies in the world would also change. As a man changes his own nature, so does the attitude of the world change towards him. This is the divine mystery supreme. A wonderful thing it is and the source of our happiness. We need not wait to see what others do.

— Mahatma Gandhi

"If they would just straighten up, I'd be happy."

"If they would treat me right, everything would be better."

"If *someone else* did something differently, my life would finally go the way I planned."

Sound familiar?

Let's start with the obvious question: am I even in control of anything? Because if my happiness or success is always dependent on what someone else does, I'm going to be disappointed every time.

Think about it. Words like *self-worth*, *self-respect*, and *self-image*—they all start with *self.* They all start with *me.*

After going through it three times now, I consider myself somewhat of an expert on marriage. Some might say I'm more of an expert on divorce, but hey, tomayto, tomahto.

We look at others and think, *Why can't I have a perfect marriage like theirs?* But here's what I've learned: there's no such thing as a perfect marriage. Marriages aren't found; they're built. They have good days and bad days, and yes, they take work. Not exhausting, soul-crushing work, but intentional effort.

My wife used to tell me that I didn't communicate. And for the longest time, I disagreed. I *was* communicating; it just wasn't in a way that made sense to her.

Over time, I realized communication styles are a lot like Dr. Gary Chapman's *Five Love Languages*. We all give and receive differently. Communication works the same way. What makes perfect sense in my head might not register at all for someone else, especially in a relationship.

For me, the problem wasn't silence; it was *too many words.*

The Godfather (my sponsor and guide through much of this journey) used to stop me mid-conversation and say, "You talk too much.You're always trying to justify, argue, defend, or explain. It's exhausting." (That's JADE, by the way — a recovery acronym that hit a little too close to home.)

One day, after another long-winded explanation, he said, "If you stopped talking so much, your life would improve."

I wanted to hang up on him. "How dare he?" I thought. "What a pompous ass."

But about a week later, I experienced an illuminating moment. I was frustrated. I felt like nothing in my marriage was improving. I needed clarity, a plan, a timeline.

After snapping at my wife as I searched for answers, she looked at me and said,

"Have the last two weeks not been good? I really thought we were making progress."

I blinked. "We haven't spoken in two weeks!"

And then it hit me.

I called the Godfather and laughed. "You were right. My life and my marriage improved the minute I stopped talking so much. I didn't go silent; I just stopped rambling to prove a point or hear my voice."

It wasn't that my wife didn't want me to speak; it was that I needed to communicate better. Fewer words. Less defense. More understanding.I didn't need to shut down; I needed to grow up.

It all had to start with *me.*

As Gandhi's quote is often paraphrased: *Be the change you wish to see in the world.*

Or to quote a different philosopher:

> *I'm starting with the man in the mirror. I'm asking him to change his ways.*
>
> — Michael Jackson

Everything I want to change out there? It begins right here.
So let it begin with me.

Chapter 4

Stay in Your Lane

When everything is coming your way, you're probably in the wrong lane.

— Tom Snyder

When we veer out of our lane, we inevitably end up in conflict with others or with ourselves. And when we obsess over what others are doing or how they're doing it, peace becomes almost impossible to find.

But is it really our business?

It's easier to judge others than it is to face our own flaws; maybe *that's* why we wander into their lane. It's less painful to focus on someone else's wrongs than to confront ours.

Like, sure, I'll call you out for deleting texts while conveniently forgetting I've done the same. I might even say, "It's different when I do it."

Classic.

If you've ever cracked open a bible or sat through Sunday School, you've probably heard the story of the woman caught in adultery. She was dragged before Jesus, accused, and according to law, was to be stoned.

Jesus was backed into a corner: follow the law and condone her death, or go against it and let her go.

His response?

"Let the one among you who is without sin cast the first stone" (John 8:7).

And in an instant, her accusers dropped their rocks and backed away because none of them were without fault. They were quick to pass judgment until they turned that judgment inward.

The truth is, we're *all* guilty of something. None of us is perfect. So what gives me the right to judge what someone else does or how they do it? Before I even consider stepping into their lane, I need to take a long look at mine.

And let's be honest; mine has potholes, wreckage, and a few traffic cones lately.

For a long time, I was quick to call people out. "She did this." "He said that." But somewhere along the way, I started to pause, and I realized, *I've done things just as bad, maybe worse.*

I couldn't, in good conscience, continue to throw the first stone.

Grant me the wisdom to know it's me.

I'm the only one I can change. I can't reroute someone else's GPS. That's not my job. Even if I'm tempted to believe I know what's "right" for them, do I really?

Look where my "best thinking" has gotten me.

There were so many times I condemned someone for their actions, only to later realize it didn't affect me at all; it just wasn't what *I* would've done.

Other times, it *did* affect me.

They were swerving all over life's highway, headed straight for a head-on collision with me. And in my infinite wisdom, I thought yelling at them would help.

"What's this moron doing?! Just turn the wheel and get back in your lane!"

"Who even *drives* like this? Probably a woman." (Sorry, ladies.)

But here's the truth: sometimes people are on a crash course, and no matter how loud I yell, I can't stop it.

The smarter move? *Get out of the way.*

Protect your peace.

Avoid the wreck.

Joy isn't about fixing everyone around me. Joy comes from *within me.*

If my joy depends on whether she has more sex with me, or he pays me more money, or they validate my feelings, then I'm chasing happiness from "sex and checks." And those will never be enough.

I've spent the last few years working on *my* side of the street: 12-step meetings, therapists, coaches, counselors, prayer, meditation (I still can't get my mind to shut up for that one). My lane's not perfect, but it's cleaner than it used to be, and I'm still sweeping.

I've also learned that when I let those practices slide, it's easy for my lane to get messy again.

As I write this, I'm still cleaning up after my own unhealthy habits, such as spending, pornography, and other dopamine-fueled distractions. I'm in no position to judge anyone else. I've got plenty of traffic to deal with right here.

And yet, that's where the growth happens. **Here. In my lane.**

And it is also in this lane where peace lives.

So back to my lane I go—with serenity to accept what I can't change, courage to change what I can, and wisdom to remember that it's *me*.

Sometimes I *do* have to swerve to avoid a collision. Because the only safe move is to get out of someone else's way.

I might lay on the horn or flip the bird on the way past to make myself feel better, but mostly, I just need to keep going.

This road is short. Spending it staring into someone else's lane doesn't make the ride longer; it just makes it less joyful.

So let other people be themselves. Let them drive how they drive. Swerve if you must. And, above all, stay in your own lane.

Chapter 5

Attitude

It is not your aptitude, but your attitude that determines your altitude.

— Zig Ziglar

They say the brain can't process negatives. If I tell you *not* to think about a giraffe...what pops into your mind?

Exactly. A giraffe.

As someone who attempts golf more than he should, I'm painfully familiar with this concept. I hear:

"Don't overswing."

"Don't slice it."

"Don't hit it in the water."

And what happens? Overswing. Slice. Splash.

Instead of focusing on the fairway, I'm mentally aiming for all the places I *don't* want to go. It's no surprise that's exactly where I end up.

This principle doesn't just apply to golf. It applies to everything.

Where our thoughts go, our energy follows.

If I spend all day stewing on my spouse's flaws, I lose sight of their strengths and the reasons I chose to build a life with them.

If I'm irritated that my kid is taking apart the remote control, I miss the wonder that he's curious and wants to understand how the world works.

An attitude of gratitude doesn't just feel good; it *works*. But so often, we do the opposite.

We focus on what we lack. We dwell in what's broken. We spiral into "woe is me."

Life becomes exhausting. Everyone's out to get us.

I challenged the guys I work with in recovery. For seven days, find one person a day to genuinely compliment. It can be a stranger, a coworker, or your kid. Be sincere. Be specific.

But I didn't tell them the catch: complimenting others helps *you* as much as it helps them.

I heard it said once, "Kindness is like perfume; you can't spray it on others without getting a little on yourself."

When you begin *looking* for what's good in others, you start to see what's good in yourself too.

You shift your lens. You stop criticizing and start appreciating.

Think about the people you know who constantly tear others down, saying: "Look at her hair." "His teeth." "Her husband's such a loser."

It doesn't end there. Now listen to how they talk about themselves: "I'm so fat." "I'm a failure." "I'm a terrible parent."

People who constantly criticize others are often reflecting *their* inner dialogue.

But when you choose to focus on the positive—when you *speak* life—you create space for growth.

I remember hearing a woman speak about her husband with such admiration. And I thought, "Why doesn't my wife talk about me like that?"

And then the hard questions hit:

Am I living in a way that inspires that kind of praise? Am I being the best person I *could* be? Or just the one I'm comfortable being? By extension, when I wish someone around me were a good spouse, friend, leader, or employee, I have to ask myself if I am being the same. I want a good spouse, but am I being a good husband? I wish I had a better co-worker, but am I being one? Before I can request something of another, I must first be one.

I wasn't showing up the way I wanted to and how she needed. I wasn't always grateful. I focused on everything I didn't have, and in the process, I became someone I didn't like very much.

So if you're reading this and felt, at any point, that I was negative toward you, let me be the first to say: *I'm sorry.*

I didn't always show up as the best husband, father, friend, or man I could be. I let the negatives cloud my vision. I lost sight of the blessings. And when you do that long enough, you forget who you are.

But gratitude changes things.

So I'll ask you what I ask myself now, daily:

Have you said something kind to someone today?

Have you told them you appreciate them?

Have you paused long enough to count your blessings?

If not, start now. Because your attitude won't just change your altitude; it might just change someone else's too.

PART III

Who's Driving Your Life?

Once we stop blaming and start reflecting, we have to ask another question: Who or what has been in the driver's seat of my life? Fear, people-pleasing, toxic relationships—it's easy to hand over the wheel. This part is about reclaiming control, learning detachment, and setting some boundaries in the rearview mirror.

Chapter 6

What Will the Neighbors Think?

You have no responsibility to live up to what other people think you ought to accomplish. I have no responsibility to be like they expect me to be. It's their mistake, not my failing.

— Richard P. Feynman

Some of the most damaging messages we carry into adulthood start in childhood, and many sound a lot like this:

"What will the neighbors think?"

"What will their parents think?"

"What will people at church say?"

That quiet (or sometimes loud) voice of societal shame often came from someone we trusted—usually a parent or caregiver who meant well. They weren't cruel. They were likely repeating the same fears someone once handed them.

Take the classic example: Always wear clean underwear in case you're in an accident. That's not about hygiene; it's about embarrassment. It's about how *you* reflect on *them.*

This people-pleasing fear follows us into adulthood, and for many of us, it grows into full-blown anxiety.

"What will people think if I don't have a designer purse?" "What will they say if I drive an old car?" "What if I'm not good enough?"

We waste our lives chasing approval from people who aren't even paying attention.

One night, someone close to me was in a drunken rage and told me I was a horrible, worthless father, my daughters didn't deserve me, and I wasn't even human garbage; I was below it. And for a moment, I believed it. For a second, it hurt.

Then I remembered what the Godfather asked me:

"Why give power to someone else's opinion, especially when it's coming from pain or projection?"

Think about it, if I told you that you're a giraffe, does that make you one? Do you grow spots? A long neck? Are you suddenly reaching for leaves?

Of course not. Because my opinion—however passionately delivered—doesn't define you.

So why do we give so much weight to the ugly opinions of others?

Here's the truth: people often project their insecurities onto others. When someone criticizes your parenting, it's usually because they're wrestling with their own feelings of inadequacy. When they attack your appearance, it's often a mirror of their self-loathing. What we dislike in others is often a reflection of what we can't face in ourselves.

That's why it's so important to check our own side of the street.

Listen closely to what someone says about others; it often reveals how they feel about themselves. Jealousy, bitterness, insecurity leak out, and if we're not careful, we absorb them.

But here's the key: what someone else thinks of you is their business, not yours.

When we live our lives constantly chasing external approval, we'll never be at peace. The goalposts keep moving. No matter how much we do, say, or earn—it's never enough for the wrong audience.

Let's talk about *FEAR* for a second. In recovery, we say it stands for:

Future **E**vents **A**ppearing **R**eal. Or: **F**alse **E**vidence **A**ppearing **R**eal.

Either way—it's not real. It's all imagined. It's anxiety about things we can't control.

Take something simple like wearing a suit. If I wear one because I *like* how I look and feel in it, that's great. But if I wear it, hoping people will *like* me more? Well, I've already lost because some people *hate* suits.

And others think you're arrogant for wearing one. So now what?

Here's the better question: **Am I wearing this for me or for them?**

When I started owning my decisions—not for approval, but for *integrity*—everything changed. I missed a lot of time with my daughters while chasing things I thought would make me happy. I chose work, distraction, and self-indulgence. I can't get that time back, but I *can* show up differently for my son and daughters, as well as myself, my spouse, and my grandchildren.

Not because I want praise or to fix the past. But because I finally understand what matters.

Let's clear up something else while we're here:

Self-care is not selfishness.

I used to confuse the two, especially when it came to my wife. There were things she did that used to frustrate me until I realized they were *healthy*.

Self-care is physical and emotional care. And when I shifted my lens, I started supporting those things she did, not resenting them.

Someone once said to me, "Paul, it's weird how many meetings you go to. People think it's strange." But my recovery isn't about other people's opinions. It's about doing what I need for *my* mental health.

And what's *weird* to others might be *life-saving* for me.

As long as our actions are healthy, harmless, and respectful of boundaries—we don't need anyone else's approval.

The real question is: Are we doing what's best for us? Or are we hiding behind the label of self-care to justify selfishness?

I've done both. I've convinced myself certain things were about finding happiness when, in reality, they were about escaping responsibility. And those choices hurt the people I loved.

So take time to examine your motives.

Is what you're doing truly nourishing your soul?Or just numbing the discomfort?

When we start choosing growth, healing, and integrity over performance, we stop living in fear of what others think.

We start defining our own value. And we start building healthier relationships, grounded in truth—not fear.

So let the neighbors think what they want. Let them judge. Let them gossip. You've got more important things to do—like living your life.

CHAPTER 7

BAD COMPANY CORRUPTS GOOD CHARACTER

Tell me with whom you associate, and I will tell you who you are.

— Johann Wolfgang von Goethe

Are we influenced by the people around us? Do the voices we allow into our lives shape the direction of our days? The answer, whether we like it or not, is a loud *yes.*

Who we surround ourselves with matters. What we consume physically, mentally, and emotionally matters. Who and what we give access to will either guide us forward or hold us back.

This is why it's so critical to examine the company we keep.

Are they challenging me to grow? Are they pushing me toward my goals? Or are they cheering me on as I drift off course, saying things like, "You're fine the way you are," even when I'm clearly not?

I once heard this simple truth:

Hang around five millionaires, and you'll probably become the sixth. Hang around five junkies... and you probably know how that ends.

Let that sit for a second.

Are the people in your life motivating you or enabling you?

Are your habits sharpening your focus or dulling your drive?

Some people, often without even realizing it, are so stuck in their own pain or fear of growth that they'll sabotage the development of others. Not because they're evil, but because your progress threatens their comfort zone. If you rise, it forces them to face the fact that they *could* change, but aren't.

You'll hear it masked as teasing.

"Why are you working so hard?" "What are you trying to prove?" "Who do you think you are?"

But let's be honest. That's not support. That's insecurity dressed up as sarcasm.

This is where *boundaries* become essential. Not walls. Not ultimatums. Not attempts to control others.

Healthy boundaries.

Dr. Henry Cloud, whose work on boundaries[1] changed my perspective entirely, put it best: "Boundaries are for your protection—not to change someone else's behavior."

A boundary is not saying, "You're not allowed to treat me that way." That's control.

A boundary is, "If you continue to treat me that way, I won't allow you access to my life."

It's like owning a piece of property. I can't stop my neighbor from trashing their yard, but I can shut my gate when their trash starts blowing into mine.

I don't have to hate them. I don't have to fight them. I simply don't let them in.

You can have lots of friends; some you're deeply aligned with, others you're not. But *you* decide who enters your inner circle. Who gets close? Who earns that access?

Someone dear to me once surrounded themselves with people who weren't going anywhere. Sure, they were fun. They had charisma. But they weren't building anything. They weren't growing. And more importantly, they weren't encouraging *anyone else* to grow either. They weren't toxic because they were cheaters, liars, or addicts. They were toxic because they were *comfortable staying stuck and pulling others back to that same place.*

That was a line I couldn't cross. It cost me some relationships, and it still causes tension in others. But it was the right line to draw.

There's an old saying:

Never wrestle with a pig. You both get dirty—and the pig likes it.

I don't need to argue with people who are determined to stay stuck. I need to surround myself with people who are determined to grow.

Let's zoom out even more.

It's not just *who* you let in. It's *what* you let in.

What you eat affects your physical health. You don't need a degree to know that eating fast food three times a day will wreck your body.

But the same principle applies to your mind.

What are you feeding your spirit? Are you constantly around people who gossip? Who tear others down? Who speak harshly about themselves and about you?

Because you *will* absorb that negativity. Even if you think you're immune, you're not.

We become what we consume.We reflect what we tolerate.We attract what we entertain.

So ask yourself:

1. Who are the five closest people to me?

2. Are they lifting me up or dragging me down?

3. What am I listening to, watching, and repeating in my head?

4. Does it build me into who I want to become?

The answers might sting. But the truth has a funny way of setting us free.

CHAPTER 8

LIVE AND LET LIVE

You can like the life you're living.You can live the life you like.

— "Nowadays," from the musical Chicago

Let them live.

Let people live the life they want—after all, **we're not the ones who have to live with the consequences of their choices**. What someone else does—or thinks, especially about me—is none of my business.

So why do we get so caught up in other people's lives? Why do we feel the need to suggest how they should live when we're not even living the life we want?

I always wanted to be a writer. Ever since I was a kid, I've loved painting pictures with words. I explored poetry, songs, erotica, general ponderings—even the occasional technical paper. But that dream? Still unfulfilled.

"One day, when I grow up, I'm going to write a book." That wasn't childhood me talking. That was forty-five-year-old me.

I spent years advising others on how they should live, but I wasn't living any of that. In fact, I'm not sure I was really living at all.

It was time to step down from my self-appointed role as CEO of other people's lives and start running my own. It was time to let go of the idea that if others didn't live the way I thought they should, my life would somehow fall apart.

But I can't control anyone. I can't make people want what I want. I love butter pecan ice cream. Some people prefer vanilla. They're not wrong. They're just happy with their preference. And instead of trying to convert them to butter pecan, maybe I should just enjoy mine while it lasts.

I had learned to Let Live—but I forgot that I, too, needed to Live.

Letting people do their thing eventually became easy. Saying, "Whatever makes you happy," became second nature.

But doing what made me happy? That was the hard part.

Would people think I was selfish? Would they judge me?Would they think less of me?

Who cares?

This life is one shot. One blink. Earth has been here for 4.5 billion years. My forty-something years are barely a blip.

Why waste them?Why miss it? Why not enjoy it? Why not live?

Once I accepted that people will do what they're going to do, no matter what I think, I found peace. I was less upset. Less bothered. Less obsessed with fixing people who weren't mine to fix.

I had to let them be. I had to accept them as they are, not as some version I wished they would become. That meant giving up the illusion of control.

And honestly? Life got better.

Some people became more enjoyable once I stopped trying to change them. Others became easier to walk away from once I saw them clearly.

Either way, I was finally free to live my life.

PART IV

Relationships in Recovery

Relationships don't magically improve at the same rate we do, but they do get more honest. Whether we're staying in the relationship, leaving it, or rebuilding it, this section explores the messy, beautiful reality of loving others while learning to love ourselves.

CHAPTER 9

SHOULD I STAY OR SHOULD I GO?

Should I stay or should I go now? If I go, there will be trouble?
And if I stay it will be double? So come on and let me know[2]
— The Clash

One of the questions I've been asked most often over the past few years is: **Should I stay, or should I go?**

For some, it's a clear-cut decision. Cross a boundary, and they're out.

But for many of us, it's not that simple. We don't just see things for what they are; we see what they could be. What we *hope* they'll become. What might happen, if only...

I have found other people's advice on relationships isn't always helpful, and I asked myself why. They have lived longer, been in more relationships, and experienced more struggles. But there's no magic answer. And as much as we want clarity from others, seeking advice from close friends and family can frequently complicate things more than it helps.

You'll hear lines like:

"If they did that to me, I'd leave in a heartbeat."

"You don't deserve that. Just walk away."

What's rarely acknowledged is this: Those same people have probably endured years of pain, dysfunction, even abuse—things far worse than what you're asking about. But it's easier to tell someone else what *they* should do than to act on the truth in your own life.

And besides, they don't have to live with the consequences. You do.

They don't know the full picture. The kids. The finances. The history. The love.

And maybe—just maybe—things aren't quite as bad as they seem in your own spinning mind.

So take outside opinions for what they are: Input, not instruction. Perspectives, not prescriptions.

Why do we feel the need to immediately make a decision? Why do we believe everything must be perfect before we take the next step?

The truth is simple. If you are standing in the fire, you move. First, you get safe, then you heal. After that, you decide. But if you are not in immediate danger, it is often wiser to slow down, breathe, and let yourself heal before choosing anything.

Decisions made from hurt rarely take us where we want to go. Often it's because we're still reacting from a place of fear, anger, or hurt. That's why *healing first* is key.

That's what I did, or at least tried my best to.I worked the steps. I saw therapists. I listened to the wisdom of the Godfather and others I trusted. I started cleaning up *my* side of the street.

When I stopped viewing the other person through a lens of resentment and started seeing them with love and acceptance—*as they are, not who I wanted them to be*—I could finally make a clear-headed decision. Whether to stay or go, I did it out of *love* for myself, not hatred toward them.

That was the turning point.

If I leave because I love myself and know I've tried everything, that's not failure. If I stay because I love myself and see the possibility of healing, that's not weakness.

Part of "trying everything" includes counseling. Let me be clear, especially to the men reading this. Counseling is not optional. It is essential. Maybe that support comes from a pastor, maybe a therapist, maybe a dominatrix who holds the keys to magically unlock the handcuffs of your life.

The point is this: It may take one person or a whole team to help you keep moving. Do not be ashamed. Do not convince yourself it is not worth it. Because it's worth every second and every penny.

Finding a therapist for myself was one of the best decisions I ever made. Couples counseling is also crucial; if your partner refuses to seek any help, that's a red flag worth paying attention to. A damaged relationship can't be rebuilt alone. You don't fix a cracked foundation by patching drywall.

In my third—yes, *third*—marriage, I gave it everything I had.I owned my mistakes.I looked at my baggage.I worked on my toxic habits.

Was I perfect? No. But I gave it everything I had.And that matters.

Hindsight shows me clearly now what it looks like when only one person is committed to healing. You can't do this work for someone else. You can only do it for yourself.

Stop trying to build a relationship based on potential. We fall in love with the future version of someone and ignore the present. But real connection only grows in the truth of today.

This is also why it's so important not to ignore red flags early on. Not to convince yourself that someone will change. Not to project your *ideal version* of them onto the reality in front of you.

Guilty as charged.

I once joked, "Yeah, I saw the red flags, but they looked like a carnival. And carnivals are fun!"

Truth is, I didn't enforce my boundaries. I didn't shut the gate when I should have. Instead, I tried to *mold* someone into the version of them I thought they should be. And we both ended up miserable.I created my own pain.

So, once again, I ask you, "Should you Stay or should you go?"

Unless there's physical or sustained emotional abuse, here's what I'd advise: Take a moment, breathe, and let yourself heal.

Work on *you* first. Accept the others for who they are, not who you want them to become. And when your heart is clear and your mind is calm, the answer will come, and it will ring loudly and clearly like a bell.

Whether you stay or go, it won't be out of fear. It'll be out of love. And the decision, and its consequences, will be yours to own.

Pause. Breathe. Heal.

Chapter 10

Teamwork

Sometimes we have to do things we don't want to do because it's the right choice. But occasionally we have to put ourselves first.

— Katherine Allred

One of my favorite sayings is: "Teamwork makes the dream work."

My son hears this all the time. My daughters used to as well. It's more than a phrase in our home; it's a way of life. Because the truth is, it takes a team to make a family function.

Sorry to disappoint anyone, but a mom can't do it all on her own, and neither can a dad. As the old saying goes, "It takes a village."

I grew up poor in rural Western Tennessee, raised mostly by a single mother. Men were in and out of our lives at different points, but that's a story for another time. For the most part, it was Mom, Amy, Daniel, and me relying on each other.

Section 8 housing, check. Government assistance, check. Not knowing what we'd eat next, check. Yet somehow, we always had enough. Our mom worked hard to make sure we did.

But she couldn't do it alone. If my brother and sister hadn't stepped in, the wheels would have fallen off the bus. Had Daniel thrown his hands up and said, "That's not my job," or "I don't want to help," things would have been very different. It took all of us to work together to keep things moving forward.

Because of that season, I learned how to cook, clean, do laundry, wash dishes, sew a button, replace a toilet, mow the yard, plant flowers, and fix the car. Life skills I still carry today. And because I can, I often DO. Especially when my partner is sick, tired, or just needs a break. (But if I'm totally honest, sometimes I find it easier to pay someone to do it, and sometimes I'm just lazy.)

When Kristin and I started dating, she told me she couldn't cook. My response, which hasn't changed, was, "That's okay because I LOVE to do it."

Cooking for others is my love language. For the record, I will also state that she is a great cook, even though, in her mind, she believes she is not. But that is not the point; **no one person should be stuck doing everything.** If you want your family to run like a well-oiled machine, it must be a team effort.

Our son repeats "teamwork makes the dream work" more than anything else because we drive that point home constantly. If we want the *dream* of a connected, joyful family, then everyone has to do their part.

I'll be honest, there was a time when I got frustrated whenever my wife took a long bath or sneaked in a nap. I'd think: *Why am I always working while she rests?*

But over time, I realized she wasn't being selfish, she was practicing self-care. She knew if she didn't prioritize time for herself, it would never happen.

She wasn't ashamed to ask for it, and neither should we be.

I still struggle with asking for time for myself, but I'm getting better. I've learned that if you don't ask, the answer is always no. And I try to offer her that space too. Something as simple as,

"You've worked hard this week. Want to take an hour for a bath while I watch the kids?"

That's teamwork.

You're both caring for each other and for the shared mission: Two healthy, happy adults raising a child who understands that *he's part of the team too.*

That's right—kids should be part of the team and not just passengers along for the ride.

We model this behavior with our son. When one of us needs time, we include him:

"Mommy had a long week. Let's help her make a bubble bath."

Now he asks for candles and bubbles when he wants to "relax" too. He's learning by example that self-care isn't selfish, it's normal.

Someone once asked, after hearing about his bath rituals, if I thought he was spoiled. I looked at him and said, "No, all kids smell that way."

But seriously, let kids see you support each other. Let them help. Let them be part of the village. They'll grow into people who support others and will ask for support when they need it.

I'll say this as much for myself as for anyone else: Stop trying to do it all. Ask for help. You're not failing, you're building a team. Be clear about what you need. No one's a mind reader, and people will only give what they're willing or able to in that moment.

And the kids? Include them. Teach them. Of course, it'll take longer. Yes, they'll slow you down. And yes, you'll have to redo some things. But that's not a burden, it's the process. And it's worth taking the time to do it right.

My son has helped me build a fence and a shed, change a light fixture, replace a dishwasher, and fix a toilet. He knows the difference between Teflon tape for pipes and electrical tape for wires. Could I have done all those things faster alone? Sure. But I would've missed the *time.* The laughter. The lessons.

That's the purpose of letting them help. You won't always get the process correct; I certainly don't. But progress is greater than perfection. And when everyone works together, even imperfectly, the resentment fades. The connection grows. The dream stays alive.

So repeat it with me (and maybe with your kids):

Teamwork makes the dream work.

Chapter 11

Courage to Change

God grant me the serenity to accept the things I cannot change, the courage to change the things I can, and the wisdom to know the difference.

— Serenity Prayer

Almost everyone has heard of the Serenity Prayer.But if you've ever worked a 12-step program, or walked through serious recovery of any kind, those words don't just sound nice. They hit *hard.* They become oxygen.

In my own journey, I've discovered something profound:

Serenity is always available when I choose acceptance.

There's a line in the Big Book that punched me right in the chest the first time I read it:

Acceptance is the answer to all my problems today. When I am disturbed, it is because I find some person, place, thing, or situation... unacceptable to me, and I can find no serenity until I accept that... as being exactly the way it is supposed to be at this moment. Nothing, absolutely nothing, happens in God's world by mistake.[3]

That paragraph taught me something I wasn't ready to admit: I can't control most of what happens around me—but I *try* to. I try hard.

When the Godfather told me I was controlling, I laughed. I mean, me? Controlling? Nah, I'm easygoing. Laid back. Not a micromanager. Not bossy. Surely not controlling.

But I was.

I wanted everything and everyone to work according to *my* plan. If only they'd listen, if only they'd behave, if only they'd do what I thought was best, then everything would be fine.

Which is funny to me now because my life, at the time, was a dumpster fire.

Eventually I had to confront the truth: The only person I could actually change was the man staring back at me in the mirror.

It wasn't *them*. It wasn't *those* situations.It wasn't my wife, my coworkers, my past, or my kid banging a toy on the table.

It was me.

That's where the **courage** comes in. Because acceptance isn't just about letting go of control. It's about taking *full ownership* of the one thing that's actually mine to manage: *myself.*

I had to stop pointing fingers and start doing the difficult, slow work of inner transformation. Was I perfect at it? Not even close, and I'm Still not. But most importantly, I started.

I will never pretend to know what another person must do to heal, but I do know what worked in my life. I know how I got here and if you follow this far, so do you.

One afternoon my wife had a group of ladies over. I baked a cake for them to enjoy while they talked and shared life around the table. It was a simple cake. Nothing exotic. Nothing you could not buy at any grocery store. The recipe shifted slightly every time I made it, but the base stayed the same, and it always came out delicious. Moist, balanced, and just sweet enough to make you close your eyes for a moment. It was the kind of cake my grandmother would have bragged about.

One woman could not stop talking about it, saying it was the best cake she had ever tasted. She praised everything about it—texture, flavor, balance. She asked me what the secret was, so I told her. The recipe was ordinary except for one thing. I added a touch of nutmeg. The original recipe did not include it. None of the recipes I researched included it. But that one little pinch gave the cake a spark that set it apart.

The moment I said "nutmeg," her whole expression changed. "NUTMEG? Who puts nutmeg in a cake? We do not believe in nutmeg in my house."

She took the recipe, marched home, and for weeks, tried to recreate the cake, all while refusing to add that one ingredient. Her cakes were good. I would have served them proudly. But they never had that something extra she tasted that day.

She wanted what I had. She wanted the flavor. She wanted the result. But the moment she heard how I got there, she shut down and rejected my answer. That is exactly what recovery often looks like. People want what you have, but fight against the idea of doing what you did.

- I want a sober life, but I still want to drink with my friends.
- I want peace, but I do not want God, and I can give you a dozen reasons why no one else should want Him either.

- I want your cake, but I am not putting nutmeg in it.

This truth ties it all together: You can make a good cake without nutmeg, but you cannot make my cake without it. In the same way, you can live a life without God, but you cannot live my life without Him.

Nutmeg is not the point. The point is this—if you want what someone else has, do not reject the ingredient that made it possible.

Putting the right ingredients together also shifted the way I parent.

Consider a five-year-old banging a toy on the table.I can tell him to stop. Will he? Maybe. Or maybe he'll look me dead in the eyes and hit it one more time—just to see what happens. (Sound familiar?)

I can't *control* his behavior, but I can influence it.I can also set boundaries and consequences, and follow through.

"You're free to hit the table. But if you choose that, I'll need to take the toy away, so the table doesn't get ruined."

That's a boundary. That's influence. That's not control.

And when he finds something *else* to test the table with five minutes later, well, I'll leave that chapter for a parenting expert (which I am *definitely* not).

The overall point I want to make in this chapter is that: Serenity doesn't come from other people behaving better.

It doesn't come from the world bending to our plans. It comes from learning to accept what *is*,change what *we can*, and stop wasting energy on what we can't.

So let me ask you the questions I had to ask myself:

- Do you have the courage to look honestly at the person in the mirror?

- Do you have the wisdom to know that person is the only one you can truly change?

Because if you do, then I promise you:

The precious gift of serenity is waiting—just on the other side of that mirror.

Serenity is always available when we choose acceptance.

Chapter 12

Grace

The moment of surrender is not when life is over. It's when life begins.

— Marianne Williamson

I almost didn't write this chapter.

For a while, I wasn't sure where it fit, or if it even belonged. But maybe the delays in finishing this book weren't random. Maybe I couldn't publish until I added this piece. Maybe this was the part I didn't know was missing until now.

It's another First Things First moment. One I didn't see coming.

It was Easter Sunday. We were sitting in our new church, listening to Pastor Dusty preach. I didn't expect the message to hit the way it did, but it stayed with me. All day. All week.

For a few years, I'd been using words like "spiritual journey" and "spiritual growth." And it was true; my mind had found more peace. My life had gained clarity. I had made progress.

But something still wasn't right.

The next day, sitting in my chair, browbeaten by the words from the previous day, I asked myself the question that had been simmering under the surface for years:

What's holding me back?

I didn't want to admit the answer. I didn't want to give up certain pieces of me: old habits, comfort zones, fragments of control. I knew that fully turning my life over meant letting go of things I wasn't ready to release.

But could I live honestly if I didn't?

Could I become the man I claimed I wanted to be if I still clung to parts of the old one?

Then, in a quiet moment, I said the words out loud.

"I surrender."

Just two words. The simplest sentence I've ever spoken, and the most difficult. And yet, the most powerful.

Revisiting *Courage to Change* now, I see the difference in who I was then versus who I am now. I understand what full surrender really feels like and what it makes possible.

That surrender didn't just change me. It reached beyond me.

Our son walks around the house singing worship songs. He prays before bed. He wants to help others, and he cares deeply. And my wife? She's showing up every day as the woman she always said she wanted to be. (Well, almost every day. Some days, she's still my little dragon.)

In 2024, my wife and I were baptized and gave our lives to Christ.

Since then, we've done our best to serve—to give, grow, and be the light in dark places. I still mess up. I still need to work on my sense of humor and my choice of words. But my heart? It's clean. It's full. And it has nowhere to go but out.

At a men's Power Lunch one afternoon, John Earle, the former NFL offensive lineman, spoke. If you ever get the chance to hear him—jump on it. He's powerful.

He shared a story of being rushed to the ER. His heart had stopped. When the doctors stabilized him, one of them said, "You were 99 percent dead."

But John's voice rang out, full of fire:

"Look what Jesus did with that 1 percent!"

That story wouldn't leave me alone.

I hadn't had a heart attack. I wasn't a former professional athlete. I wasn't an evangelist leading crowds to Christ. But still, it hit me like a freight train. I couldn't shake it.

Weeks later, I approached John at another event and told him how much that story had stuck with me. I shared a bit of our story: our son singing worship songs, finishing Bible stories at dinner from memory. My wife thriving in PTA, plants growing like a jungle. Our marriage is deepening. Our son is flourishing. My career is gaining momentum.

But just a few years before, we experienced infidelity. Alcoholism. Arguments. Anger. Nights sleeping in separate rooms. Silent dinners. Two people barely speaking; living for themselves, not for each other. Not for God.

I had the divorce papers on my desk.

One signature would've ended it.

We were 99 percent done.

But look what Jesus did with that 1 percent!

That 1 percent didn't just save our marriage.

It began to redeem our purpose. Our home. Our legacy. And it reminded me that spiritual progress doesn't stop when life gets better. It only deepens.

The journey I thought I was on had brought me far. But surrender—that moment of capitulation—was what made the journey real. It also made me realize that I had to "go there" to "get here,"

When I finally let go of what I was holding onto, my hands were finally open to use.

PART V

THE DISCIPLINE OF NOW

It's hard to remain in the present. Our minds drift to what was or what might be. But healing requires us to return, again and again, to the ground under our feet. These chapters are about presence, priorities, and learning how to be where you are.

Chapter 13

Time Will Pass

Time is free, but it's priceless. You can't own it, but you can use it. You can't keep it, but you can spend it. Once you've lost it you can never get it back.

— Harvey Mackay

One of the best life lessons I ever learned came long before this season of growth—on a mat, wearing a gi.

I was learning Brazilian Jiu-Jitsu, but more than that, I was learning *about myself*. Not just from coaches and teammates, but also from the guys choking me out on the mat.

To this day, I still can't complete a choke to submission. But the lessons I took away from those hours in training. They've stuck with me far longer than any submission ever did.

For example, I used to think that I didn't need help; others do.

That Jiu-Jitsu lesson came rushing back to me recently while talking with someone new to a recovery program. They were where I once was—hurt, angry, and *absolutely certain* they weren't the problem.

"I don't need this. THEY need help. Look what THEY did to me!"

I remember that mindset. When I first dialed in to hear people share, I was MAD. I wasn't looking for homework; I was looking for answers. I wanted relief, not *steps*. Encouragement, not *meetings*. I was drowning, and they handed me a workbook.

But I stuck with it.

I met the Godfather.

I started the steps.

I read, I listened, I showed up, and little by slowly, my life got worse.

Or so it seemed.

You see, just like construction, healing requires a *demo* first. You can't build something new without tearing down what's broken first.

It was just like Jiu-Jitsu.

Back on the mat, I was prepping for my first international tournament. I was terrified.

What if I wasn't good enough? What if I lost? What if I embarrassed myself, or worse, embarrassed my team?

I thought about quitting.

That's when my coach reminded me of something simple, but powerful:

"How you use your time is your choice. Whether time passes or not, is not."

I could train or I could quit, but either way, that tournament was coming. And time would pass, regardless of what I did with it.

Same with recovery.

I could put in the work—the healing, the honesty, the rebuilding—or I could stay angry, bitter, and blame everyone else. Time would pass either way.

I lost that first match by a matter of points. But if I were honest, I got smoked. Walked off the mat with my head down, embarrassed, and ashamed, until my team met me with smiles.

One of my professors looked me in the eyes and said: "There are no losses. We either win or we learn."

That moment hit hard. I realized that I didn't *lose;* I *learned*. I learned how badly I needed to do more cardio. I learned how an adrenaline dump feels. I learned that I didn't even know what I didn't know.

And that's true in life too. We don't know what we don't know until we get in the ring and *try*.

Life gives us the same options: We can do the work, or we can make excuses. We can build something better, or we can sit in the rubble and complain. But the time?

It will pass either way.

The question is:

Will you spend it learning and growing, or looking back, wishing you had?

Time will pass regardless of your decision.

Chapter 14

First Things First

Clutter is nothing more than postponed decisions.

— Barbara Hemphill

As a father, one of my deepest hopes is to leave a lasting, positive impact on my children, to reach old age knowing I taught them lessons that shaped their lives for the better.

We spend so much time trying to mold our kids into who we want them to be, often steering them in the opposite direction of our own mistakes. We just don't want them to feel the pain we did.

But let's be honest: Did you listen to your parents? I didn't. Not until it was too late and I found myself wishing I had.

Children don't learn because we tell them what to do. They learn by what we model. They learn what they live.

There are countless lessons I wish I'd taught my daughters when they were little, but now, I focus on what I can still model for my son.

At the time I'm writing this, my son, nicknamed Turbo at birth, is a wild, brilliant force of nature. One minute he's building a Lego city, the next he's staging a fire truck rescue in a pillow fort, and by afternoon he's decorating the walls, so his stuffed animals have something pretty to look at.

It's chaos. Beautiful, imaginative chaos.

And then comes the crash.

"It's too much! It'll take FOREVER to clean up!"

Cue tears. Panic. A full meltdown over the mess he created in under twenty minutes.

One day, he asked me for help. I told him, calmly:

"First things first. Let's pick up the Legos, then the blocks, then the art stuff. One at a time."

I didn't think much of it; I was just trying to help him not spiral emotionally.

First things first. That phrase stuck, probably because I'd heard it the night before in a recovery meeting.

First things first.

I hadn't planned to repeat it. But apparently, my subconscious took over, and thank God it did.

Because the truth is, I'm the same way.

I've sat there overwhelmed by life, staring at a mess of tasks and emotional chaos, thinking:

"This is too much. It'll take forever to fix."

Whether it's work, relationships, healing, or even cleaning a kitchen, if we try to do everything at once, we shut down. But if we prioritize, if we break it down, if we focus on just the next right thing, **we start moving again.**

That's what *first things first* is about.

In sales, I know this well: Before you close a deal, you need to find the lead.

And we all know this:

Fail to plan? Plan to fail.

Same goes for parenting. For marriage. For healing. For life.

Turbo didn't just learn a better way to clean; he learned the power of a plan. And more than that, he learned to ask for help *with* a plan.

That's wildly different from just crying and expecting someone else to fix everything.

"Dad, I need to pick up the Legos first. Can you help me?"

That's not just asking for help; that's showing commitment to the solution.

How do we eat an elephant? One bite at a time.

Life can be overwhelming. So much of it comes at us at once.

Just like the Legos on his floor, we have to take life *one bite at a time.* We have to handle *first things first.*

This book should've been finished four years ago, honestly.

I didn't know why it wasn't, not until I reviewed this chapter.

I had gone back many times and made changes. Added things. Took things out. But mostly, I still had to fix *me*. I had to let go of resentment and anger. I removed stories. I changed tone. I rewrote with humility instead of bitterness.

I had to get *me* right first.

Then I could move on to the next step. And the next. And the next.

The first time I heard my son say "First things first" while cleaning, I froze.

Where had he learned that?

Then my wife said,

"Just like Daddy always says."

He had learned it from *me.*

And at that moment, I realized:

He wasn't just learning from me, he was also holding me accountable.

So what's your first thing today?

Pick it.Do it.Then do the next thing.

First things first.

Chapter 15

Be Where Your Feet Are

I, not events, have the power to make me happy or unhappy today. I can choose which it shall be. Yesterday is dead, tomorrow hasn't arrived yet. I have just one day, today, and I'm going to be happy in it.

—— Groucho Marx

I've heard it a million times: Be present. Enjoy today. Live in the now.

I understood it, at least I thought I did. But understanding a concept isn't the same as living it. And if I've learned anything in recovery, it's that knowing better doesn't always mean doing better.

For months, I found myself in meetings without knowing exactly why I was there. But more often than not, I'd hear something that punched me square in the chest. Other times, maybe it wasn't for me, but later,

I'd cross paths with someone else who *needed* it. Just like the Godfather always says, "There are no accidents."

In one of those meetings, I heard a phrase that shifted something in me almost instantly: "Be where your feet are."

As someone who can (and does) overthink everything, this statement rocked me. My mind constantly tries to live five steps ahead, or five years behind. I can be sitting on the couch with my wife and still be mentally rerunning a conversation I had with my boss. I can be pushing my son on a swing and thinking about bills, emails, deadlines, or what I should've said three days ago. I'm not where my feet are; I'm where my *fear* is.

And the irony? That kind of thinking usually ties back to things I can't control anyway.Just like I wrote in *Courage to Change*, serenity starts when I accept that I can't change the past, and I can't control people. I can only control *me*. And right now, "me" is standing on a playground, with a little boy yelling, "Dad! Watch this!"

And sometimes, I miss it.

When I'm not present, I'm not just missing the moment—I'm also fueling old insecurities. In "Should I Stay or Should I Go," I talked about how much damage overthinking and resentment can do in a relationship. Doubt, second-guessing, and wondering if I'm "enough" don't live in the now. They live in wounds. And if I want peace, I need to put *first things first* and deal with them, rather than letting them run my headspace on autopilot.

This is why *boundaries* matter too—not just with people, like I shared in "Bad Company Corrupts Good Character," but with *distractions*. Social media, texts, news alerts, stress triggers—they don't belong in every moment. There's a time to grind and a time to rest. A time to think about the budget, and a time to go down the slide with your kid. One needn't rob the other.

And speaking of that, presence isn't a solo sport; it's a *team* sport. In "Teamwork Makes the Dream Work," I talked about how much smoother life runs when everyone's doing their part. But part of being a teammate is showing up—fully. Not halfway. Not physically there but emotionally miles away. Our kids notice that. Our partners feel that. Presence *is* participation.

I even noticed how much more manageable things became for my son once we started applying *First Things First* in everyday moments. What used to send him into a spiral—cleaning up a disaster zone of blocks, pillows, crayons, and stuffed animals—now became a step-by-step process. "First, let's pick up the Legos. Then the books." We did it together. We focused on the *now*. He learned from my example, and without knowing it, held me accountable to keep modeling it.

So now, throughout the day, I ask myself:

Am I where my feet are?

When I focus on that question, I find everything slows down. Conversations get richer. Intimacy feels deeper. Laughter feels louder. Even grief or stress becomes more bearable when I don't add the weight of the future or the past.

And in case you're wondering—no, I don't get it right all the time. Sometimes I have to ask myself that question a hundred times a day. But every time I do, my answer brings me back to the present. I shut out the noise, silence the phone, and return to now.

Because *right now* is the only place life is actually happening.

Be. Where. Your. Feet. Are.

Chapter 16

Epilogue

I am still not perfect. I still fall short more often than I like to admit. But I found my way back to God. I stopped running into the dark, trying to carry a weight meant for hands stronger than mine. I stopped believing I was in control of everything. I stopped trying to rewrite my story with a broken pen that could never fix the pages I had already torn. When I finally surrendered, God met me in the wreckage and lifted what I could no longer carry.

Along the way, I had to release some relationships. Some people left gently. Others left like a storm. But looking back, I can see the grace in both situations. Not everyone is meant to walk the whole road with you. Some only hand you a piece of the map.

What matters is that I kept walking, even when I didn't know the next step or when the path was quiet or crooked. I kept going.

I've learned to carry less. I've learned to be kind—with my words, with my time, with myself. I've learned that love sometimes looks like rest, boundaries, and letting someone else take the lead for a while. I've learned to slow down and put first things first.

Most of all, I've learned presence. I don't need to chase tomorrow or drag yesterday around with me. I can stand still and listen. I can breathe and be where I am.

I am still becoming. Still healing. Still being reshaped in ways I don't fully understand.

But I know now that I was never walking alone. And grace has a longer reach than I ever imagined.

So no matter what I still don't know,or how far I still have to go...

At least now, I know where my feet are.

Acknowledgements

While there are many people thanked at the beginning of this book and others mentioned throughout, those are all people who were a part of or made the journey possible. I'm forever grateful for each of them, as well as the countless number of people not mentioned who have changed my life over the years. They each hold a place near and dear to my heart because, without them, this story wouldn't exist. But without a few others, this book wouldn't be in your hands right now.

Don Polley, you encouraged me throughout my entire life to see my potential and live up to it. In September 2023, you sent me an image with a caption that read,

> "Never give up on a dream just because of the time it will take to accomplish it. The time will pass anyway."
>
> — Earl Nightingale.

Beneath it, you wrote, "Keep working on your book! I'm anxious to read it!" I knew something was missing, but I didn't yet know what it was. Every day, without fail, until the day you passed, you sent something—an encouragement, a prayer, or a reminder to keep going. When

I wrote the chapter "Grace," I finally understood why those messages mattered more than I realized. You were the first person to push me toward this, and I'm confident this dream would never have become reality without you.

Kristin, even after meeting with the publishers, I almost didn't pull the trigger. When you looked at me after reading it and, with a smile, said, "You should publish it," that was the final nudge I needed. You always seem to know when I'm standing in my own way and how to get me moving again.

Elizabeth, not only have you been a major highlight of my life, you were the bridge to everything that happened here. You connected me to Tracy, who designed the most beautiful book cover I've ever seen. Honestly, I'd buy it just for the artwork. When I saw that cover, the book finally felt real. Then, faced with another opportunity to quit because I didn't know where to go next, Tracy connected me to Dana and Rikki. The rest was history. From the first moment we talked, I knew there was no one else I wanted to work with.

Dana, when you said, "I want to make your dream come true," it felt like Don was speaking through you, reminding me not to give up. You and Rikki brought this story to life in ways I could never have done alone.

Lori, you stepped in as my editor and became another magician behind the scenes working fervently to make sure I look good. You brought clarity to my words and strength to the message and you did it with kindness and care. Thank you for everything you poured into this project. I cannot wait to team up with all of you again on the next book coming soon.

Thank you to each and every one of you for your belief in me and your encouragement to keep going. My hope is that because of the belief so many amazing people had in me, someone out there will read this book and find their own life will have changed.

About the Author

Paul Carlson was born in Chicago and spent his formative years in rural West Tennessee. A lifelong Chicago Cubs fan, he never set out to write a book — he just had a lot to say and finally decided to say it out loud.

A dad, husband, and deeply work-in-progress human, Paul shares his story in hopes it'll help someone else find clarity in their own chaos.

He now lives in North Texas with his wife, son, and a revolving door of creative projects, unfinished home repairs, and life lessons. When he's not writing, working, or building something with Legos, he's probably in the kitchen baking sourdough goodies for his cottage bakery, Fishes & Loaves.

Where Are My Feet? is his first book—a raw, hopeful reminder that transformation doesn't begin once you have it all figured out. It begins exactly where you stand.

Endnotes

1. Cloud, Henry. "Boundaries: Why You Need Them and How to Set Them." Youtube.com. Accessed November 20, 2025. https://www.youtube.com/watch?v=RkoG6XCHPUs&t=221s .

2. The Clash. "Should I Stay or Should I Go." *Combat Rock.* CBS Records, 1982.

3. Alcoholics Anonymous: The Big Book. (New York: Alcoholics Anonymous World Services, 2001), 417.

www.ingramcontent.com/pod-product-compliance
Lightning Source LLC
LaVergne TN
LVHW090616110826
845146LV00001B/416

* 9 7 9 8 9 9 3 2 7 2 0 3 0 *